D0308018

YORK NOTES

Educating Rita

Willy Russell

Notes by Tony Rawdin

 Longman   York Press

YORK PRESS
322 Old Brompton Road, London SW5 9JH

ADDISON WESLEY LONGMAN LIMITED
Edinburgh Gate, Harlow,
Essex CM20 2JE, United Kingdom
Associated companies, branches and representatives throughout the world

First published 1998

ISBN 0–582–36827–8

Designed by Vicki Pacey, Trojan Horse, London
Illustrations by Susan Scott
Phototypeset by Gem Graphics, Trenance, Mawgan Porth, Cornwall
Colour reproduction and film output by Spectrum Colour
Produced by Addison Wesley Longman China Limited, Hong Kong

CONTENTS

PREFACE

York Notes are designed to give you a broader perspective on works of literature studied at GCSE and equivalent levels. We have carried out extensive research into the needs of the modern literature student prior to publishing this new edition. Our research showed that no existing series fully met students' requirements. Rather than present a single authoritative approach, we have provided alternative viewpoints, empowering students to reach their own interpretations of the text. York Notes provide a close examination of the work and include biographical and historical background, summaries, glossaries, analyses of characters, themes, structure and language, cultural connections and literary terms.

If you look at the Contents page you will see the structure for the series. However, there's no need to read from the beginning to the end as you would with a novel, play, poem or short story. Use the Notes in the way that suits you. Our aim is to help you with your understanding of the work, not to dictate how you should learn.

York Notes are written by English teachers and examiners, with an expert knowledge of the subject. They show you how to succeed in coursework and examination assignments, guiding you through the text and offering practical advice. Questions and comments will extend, test and reinforce your knowledge. Attractive colour design and illustrations improve clarity and understanding, making these Notes easy to use and handy for quick reference.

York Notes are ideal for:
- Essay writing
- Exam preparation
- Class discussion

The author of these Notes is Tony Rawdin, who currently works as Director of Communications at a comprehensive school in County Durham. He studied English Language and Literature at the University of Liverpool and gained his Masters Degree from the University of York.

The text used in these Notes is the Longman edition, 1991.

Health Warning: This study guide will enhance your understanding, but should not replace the reading of the original text and/or study in class.

PART ONE

INTRODUCTION

HOW TO STUDY A PLAY

You have bought this book because you wanted to study a play on your own. This may supplement classwork.

- Drama is a special 'kind' of writing (the technical term is 'genre') because it needs a performance in the theatre to arrive at a full interpretation of its meaning. When reading a play you have to imagine how it should be performed; the words alone will not be sufficient. Think of gestures and movements.

- Drama is always about conflict of some sort (it may be below the surface). Identify the conflicts in the play and you will be close to identifying the large ideas or themes which bind all the parts together.

- Make careful notes on themes, characters, plot and any sub-plots of the play.

- Playwrights find non-realistic ways of allowing an audience to see into the minds and motives of their characters. The 'soliloquy', in which a character speaks directly to the audience, is one such device. Does the play you are studying have any such passages?

- Which characters do you like or dislike in the play? Why? Do your sympathies change as you see more of these characters?

- Think of the playwright writing the play. Why were these particular arrangements of events, these particular sets of characters and these particular speeches chosen?

Studying on your own requires self-discipline and a carefully thought-out work plan in order to be effective. Good luck.

Willy Russell was born in 1947 in Whiston, just outside Liverpool. His father was a factory worker, until he gave it up to buy a fish and chip shop. His mother had a menial job in a warehouse. The young Russell, therefore, had the sort of upbringing which failed to indicate any sort of literary potential, let alone suggest a career of writing which would establish himself as one of the most popular and successful playwrights (see Literary Terms) of modern times.

Education
Notice the links between Willy Russell and Rita who both fail to succeed at school.

At school, by his own admission, Willy Russell failed to excel. He did enjoy reading though, and it was during this period of his life that he first dreamed of becoming a writer. However, believing this to be a foolish notion for someone of his class, he buried the thought deep within himself for many years. Rather like Rita in *Educating Rita*, it was only in adulthood that he could break away from the pressure of his peers and follow his own desire for education.

Early employment

After failing his Apprentice Printer's examination, Russell acted on his mother's suggestion and became a qualified ladies' hairdresser, eventually running his own small salon. He never really enjoyed this job and claims that he was never any good at it either, but on quiet days it did at least provide him with the opportunity to begin writing. This led to him passing 'O' Level English Literature at night school and a short spell working at a car factory earned him enough money to enrol full time at college. It is easy to see that there are definite parallels between his own life and the experiences of his fictional character, Rita.

Other works

Apart from *Educating Rita*, which was written in 1979, Willy Russell has written a number of other popular and successful plays such as *Breezeblock Park* (1975), *One for the Road* (1976), *Our Day Out* (1977), *Stags and Hens* (1978) and *Blood Brothers* (1981). Perhaps his most celebrated work, other than *Educating Rita*, is the play *Shirley Valentine* (1986). Both have been adapted for the cinema and turned into highly acclaimed films.

CONTEXT & SETTING

The opening of *Educating Rita* states that the events are set in a university somewhere 'in the north of England'. However, there can be little doubt that Rita's broad Scouse accent locates the play more specifically in Liverpool, Willy Russell's home town. Despite this, the play has a distinctly universal appeal. Rita reflects, at first glance, a working-class desire to escape from her own culture and background, in order to lead an apparently more fulfilling life in the type of society represented by Frank and the other students with whom she comes into contact.

The working class background

Rita claims that the working class have effectively lost their culture and all she sees are people who are 'pissed, or on the Valium, tryin' to get from one day to the next'. There appears to be no meaning to their lives. When Rita fails to find the necessary self-confidence to attend Frank's dinner party one Saturday night, she meets up with the rest of her family in the local pub instead. Although everyone appears to be happy as they all sing together, Rita senses that this is simply a thin veneer and the tears shed by her mother would appear to justify this. When Rita asks her mother why she is crying, she replies with bitter poignancy, 'we could sing better songs than those'. Clearly, this is meant to be taken **metaphorically** (see Literary Terms). Rita's mother, just like her daughter, has a clear perception that there ought to be more to life than the humdrum and rather shallow existence they are leading.

Rita's desire for change is shared by her mother, but Denny is an example of a working-class man who is apparently satisfied with his lot.

Although society has altered radically in many ways since the time when the play was written, it could be

argued that *Educating Rita* is now more relevant than
ever. The more divided that society becomes, the
greater the need for the impoverished people to escape.
Moreover, the play can be viewed on a purely personal
level. Here is a woman whose lack of fulfilment must be
shared by many people who sit in the audience and
witness Rita's attempts to change herself and her
situation. She experiences problems in her marriage,
and her husband's desire for her to have children only
throws the dilemma into sharper focus. How can Rita
have children when she knows that she is not ready for
the responsibility? She yearns for something substantial
in her life and realises that she must 'discover meself
first' before she can contemplate bringing children into
the world.

SETTING

The play is **naturalistic** (see Literary Terms) in the
sense that all the action takes place in Frank's study. By
doing so, Willy Russell is taking Rita out of her world
and immersing her in Frank's. The room itself is
significant. The fact that it is set in a Victorian-built
university suggests tradition and permanence, and even
its position on the first floor is significant as it allows
Rita literally to rise above the common mass of
humanity and look at the world from a different angle.
The rows and rows of books which dominate the stage
represent the world of knowledge to which Rita aspires
and they enable her to experience life in a variety of
forms. Although her experiences are second-hand, they
do allow Rita to change into an entirely different
person.

Academic
background

Frank's cultural background is entirely alien to Rita
when she first attends the Open University course, but
she is determined to fit in with his social and academic

Note how Rita aims to escape from her roots and fit in with Frank's circles, but she soon finds that she is comfortable in neither environment.

circles. In doing so, she proposes to alter her whole way of living. Instead of spending evenings in the pub, she chooses to visit the theatre. Her choice of books, clothes and even her job is governed by a burning desire to be accepted into Frank's world, all of which seems ironic (see Literary Terms) in view of the fact that Frank himself is certainly not happy with his own lifestyle. Divorced and now struggling to maintain a relationship with Julia, one of his ex-students, his dissatisfaction with life is reflected in his inability to write the sort of poetry he would like and a growing drink problem.

PART TWO

SUMMARIES

GENERAL SUMMARY

The play is about Rita's attempt to break free from her mundane existence as a hairdresser and enter fully and with confidence into Frank's academic, middle-class world.

Act I

In the opening moments of the play, we are made aware of Frank's drink problem. Dissatisfied with his academic career, he has turned to the bottle to forget his pain, and even before Rita arrives for her tutorial he has already contemplated a visit to the pub to 'wash away the memory of some silly woman's attempt to get into the mind of Henry James'.

Note how the development of language goes hand-in-hand with the development of character.

Rita's first, clumsy entry reflects her social inferiority. She is ill at ease and is finding it difficult to break into Frank's world. Her strong Liverpudlian accent clearly identifies her as coming from a completely different background, and her decision to change her name from Susan to Rita reflects a desire to escape her working-class roots and enter into a middle-class, academic environment represented by Frank and his regular students.

To Frank, Rita is like 'the first breath of air' that has been in his room for years, but he feels uneasy in his role as a night school tutor on the Open University course and attempts to persuade Rita to change to another tutor. However, a bond rapidly emerges between the two characters and Rita is adamant that Frank is going to be the one to educate her, because he is 'a crazy mad piss artist who wants to throw his students through the window, an' I like you'.

Rita's marriage breaks down as a result of her education, but what would have happened if Denny had supported her?

In trying to escape from one world and enter into another, Rita finds that many conflicts emerge. Her husband's lack of support means that she has to write her essays in quiet moments at work (hardly ideal conditions for study!). This conflict deepens when Denny burns her books, on finding out that Rita had been taking the contraceptive pill against his wishes. The relationship cannot sustain such conflict and, eventually, the marriage breaks down.

Throughout the first half of the play, Rita looks upon herself as a 'half-caste', neither feeling comfortable in her own world, nor possessing the confidence to mix in the social circles inhabited by Frank when he invites her to dinner at his home.

The first half of the play ends with Rita coming to a crossroads in her development. She could choose to turn the clock back and return to her former way of life, but she decides against this. Instead, she determines to press on with her education and, with renewed vigour, she is able to channel all her energy into the learning process.

Act II

As Act II gets under way, we almost immediately detect a change in the relationship between Frank and Rita. Following her success at summer school, she is brimming with confidence and she has found another sort of teacher in Trish, her new flatmate: 'She's dead classy. Y' know like, she's got taste, y' know like you, Frank, she's just got it.'

With her greater sense of comfort in this middle-class world, we witness Rita beginning to take control of her relationship with Frank. She takes the lead when suggesting that they should study 'a dead good poet', and tries to persuade Frank to have the tutorial outside on the grass.

Consider the way Rita's strength comes at the expense of Frank's security.

We now become more aware of Frank's own weaknesses. His drinking is taking such a hold upon his life that Rita is forced to warn him that 'It'll kill y', Frank'. His marriage has already broken down and his relationship with Julia seems to be under threat. At the centre of all this is Frank's inability to write the sort of poetry that he would like. A sense of failure and frustration spills over into his teaching and, possibly to escape the consequences, he turns to the whisky bottle for comfort. As Rita searches for her true self, it seems that Frank is losing his own sense of identity.

The more confident Rita becomes, the less she needs Frank. Conversely, we see that, as the play develops, Frank becomes more absorbed by Rita's character. Rather **ironically** (see Literary Terms), it is he who needs Rita's company and not the other way round. He becomes distinctly uneasy about the way Rita's character is changing and, to some extent, he is given good reason. Rita's attempt to speak 'properly' appears ludicrous and yet this has to be taken in the context of her trying to 'find' herself.

Think about the ways in which Frank makes matters worse between himself and Rita.

In the later scenes of the play, we witness their relationship breaking down. Rita is late for a tutorial and when Frank rings her at work, he finds that she has left the hairdressing salon to work in a bistro. Frank is hurt that Rita has not confided in him, but Rita simply brushes it aside as not being of any consequence. The conflict between Rita and Denny in Act I is giving way to a conflict between Rita and Frank in Act II. We see Frank, in a state of inebriation, sending Rita away to write a critical appraisal of his own poetry, and this leads to the climax of their conflict when she returns with her views the following day. Frank is scathing about Rita's lack of real learning, stating that her positive response to the poems is borne out of her pseudo-intellectual approach to the course, and that there is nothing personal in her analysis.

Between Scene 5 and Scene 6, there is evidently a time lapse. After a period of time, when Rita and Frank have not seen each other, Frank tries to make amends by ringing her to tell her about the impending examination. Another time lapse occurs just before the final scene when Rita comes to thank Frank for being a good teacher. Having passed her examination, she has the opportunity to choose her own direction in life, and Frank even asks her to accompany him to Australia, following his banishment by the university authorities.

The play ends on a lighter note with Rita preparing to give Frank a haircut. The audience is aware of the sexual undertones when Rita tells Frank 'I never thought there was anythin' I could give you. But there is. Come here, Frank ...', but Willy Russell undercuts this with the final line, 'I'm gonna take ten years off you ...'.

DETAILED SUMMARIES

ACT I

SCENE 1

The opening scene, as for the entire play, is set in a first-floor room of a Victorian-built university in the north of England.

When the curtain rises, we see Frank, who is in his early fifties, busily searching along rows of bookshelves to find a hidden bottle of whisky. Now a rather disenchanted English lecturer, he has no enthusiasm for the Open University course on which Rita has enrolled.

Rita's first entry is a clumsy affair, rattling at the door knob and unable to get in. However, there is an air of

Consider Willy Russell's use of entrances for comic effect.

determination about her which Frank finds impossible to ignore. She is like a 'breath of air', different to all the other students, and it is this freshness which is so appealing.

Note Rita's coarse and vulgar language.

When talking about the picture of a nude religious scene hanging on Frank's wall, Rita asks her tutor whether or not he thinks of it as erotic. On hearing Frank's reply, 'I suppose it is', Rita's reaction is to state, 'There's no suppose about it. Look at those tits'. This is typical of Rita and Frank's conversation as they get acquainted.

Here again is another mismatch between Rita and the academic world she is entering.

Their subjects of conversation quickly change, Rita offering Frank a cigarette and talking about people being afraid of death, which then reminds her of a poem on the same topic. Frank immediately assumes that Rita is speaking of the celebrated Welsh poet, Dylan Thomas, only to be told that she is, in fact referring to a poem by the contemporary Liverpool writer, Roger McGough. Not surprisingly, Frank has to admit, 'I don't think I know the actual piece you mean …'.

We learn that Rita's real name is Susan and that she is calling herself by this new name after Rita Mae Brown, the authoress of her favourite novel entitled *Rubyfruit Jungle*. Frank is clearly not impressed by such writing.

They then talk about E.M. Forster, the educated class life in comparison to Rita's, Yeats and Rita's learning. Rita talks about life at the hairdressers, herself and how at twenty-six, she feels 'out of step'; while everyone else is expecting her to settle down and have children in the near future, Rita wants to discover herself first.

Partly fearful of taking on such a burdensome responsibility and partly because of the course's unsocial hours that limit his drinking time, Frank encourages

Rita to change tutors. Initially, she exits only to return moments later with the command, 'you are my teacher – an' you're gonna bleedin' well teach me'. And if Frank was left in any doubt as to what he was taking on with his new student, he could not fail to realise it when Rita closes the scene with her assertion that she will cut his hair at the next meeting.

COMMENT

Note the **stage directions** (see Literary Terms) which describes the scene. Be aware of these as you are reading the play.

The first scene opens up Rita's character, enabling the audience to see why she has been driven to join the course.

Rita is attempting to create a new identity for herself. She is searching for a new meaning in her life and Frank is that means to an end. This lack of education but clear desire to learn is revealed in many ways in this scene, for instance when Rita asks Frank what **assonance** (see Literary Terms) means. Education is a way for Rita to escape from her working-class surroundings.

Rita's perceptions
of quality
literature are not
the same as
Frank's.

At this stage of Rita's development, we see that she is desperate to find herself but does not know where to begin. She obviously feels that the change of name is important and yet casual observers would recognise that this is entirely superficial.

It is the mismatch between Rita's language and the academic **setting** (see Literary Terms) that is the source of much humour in the play. Her accent and **dialect** (see Literary Terms) clearly sets her apart and so too does the constant swearing and joking. However, sometimes it is her lack of knowledge that marks the difference: 'Do you know Yeats?' says Frank. 'The wine lodge?' comes the reply.

It is interesting to note that since the play was written, Roger McGough has continued to receive wide critical acclaim. Frank is dismissive of this poet and, **ironically** (see Literary Terms), it takes Rita to indicate his true ability. Significantly, by the end of the play, the audience has become all too aware that Frank is having problems writing his own poetry and that he would give anything to be able to write as freely as McGough.

Look closely at who is in control here, and consider if this situation changes throughout the play.

Frank's own lack of confidence is highlighted in his attempt to persuade Rita to find another tutor. Although he maintains that the reason for this is because the evening course interferes with his drinking, one suspects that Frank is frightened of the challenge which faces him. Unlike most of his other students who could, by and large, get along without him, Rita is totally reliant on Frank for her education.

Rita is already beginning to find her feet to some extent. At the end of the scene Rita calls Frank a 'geriatric hippie', reflecting the confidence and security she feels in his company. Although it takes much longer for her to mix effectively with his regular students, the fact that Rita strikes up an immediate rapport with Frank is significant if she is to develop.

GLOSSARY   **Yates Wine Lodge** Rita confuses Yeats with Yates, a chain of wine bars

Yeats William Butler Yeats (1865–1939) an Irish poet – note that this play has many references to literary figures and works, as Rita is being educated. For further information look them up in any good literature encyclopedia

Rita Mae Brown an American author who wrote a sexually explicit novel *Rubyfruit Jungle*

geriatric hippie the hippies of the 1960s rejected traditional values and grew their hair long. So Frank's wild hairstyle makes him look like an ageing hippie

SCENE 2

Rita's second entrance involves Frank, along with the audience, witnessing the door handle being turned and turned again, but no one entering. When Frank finally opens the door, he reveals Rita, oil can in hand, trying to fix the faulty handle. She announces that she is doing it because she knows he will not.

Note that Rita moves restlessly about the room, trying to familiarise herself with the surroundings.

Once inside, Rita walks round Frank's room looking at various objects, admiring her tutor's taste. When she looks out of the window at the lawns, she asks Frank whether the 'proper' students sit down there to study, clearly distinguishing herself as not a 'proper' student. Rita describes how, as a child, she had a yearning to attend boarding school because of her vision of 'tuck-shop', 'matron' and 'prep'. She describes her dissatisfaction with her own schooling: 'borin', ripped-up books, broken glass everywhere, knives an' fights.' Although she jokes, 'An' that was just the staffroom', the audience senses that there is a serious issue underlying all this cheerful banter. Rita explains that although the teachers tried their best, she was unable to commit herself to her education because there was no academic atmosphere. Studying was for the 'whimps', as she puts it, and for her to take school seriously she would have had to become different to her friends.

She now considers that it was this need for conformity that led to a rather shallow existence: music, clothes and 'lookin' for a feller' seemed to be the sum total of her experience. Rita comments that buying a new dress to change the external appearance can deflect you from the need to change yourself on the inside. Now, as a symbolic (see Literary Terms) gesture, Rita is wearing an old dress and is refusing to buy another until she passes her first exam. By then, she hopes to have become an entirely new person and will be able to buy the 'sort of dress you'd only see on an educated woman'. The tutorial itself revolves around the E.M. Forster novel *Howards End*, which Rita had taken to read on her first visit. As with her appreciation of *Rubyfruit Jungle*, Rita responds to the text in a purely subjective manner, and it is Frank's task to develop in Rita a sense of critical detachment that will enable her to pass the examination.

Frank talks of Rita disciplining her mind and we see how she is unable to concentrate on the real business of the tutorial, choosing to probe into Frank's personal life instead. Here, we learn of Frank's marriage break up and his new life with Julia, his early volumes of poetry and his recent inability to write.

There is clearly a strong attraction and closeness between Frank and Rita, but Rita does her best to play it down.

Both characters open their souls and there is tension in the line, 'Rita – why didn't you walk in here twenty years ago?' but Rita extricates herself from an uncomfortable situation with the humorous retort, 'Cos I don't think they would have accepted me at the age of six'. The scene ends with Frank trying once again to focus Rita's attention on the Forster novel.

COMMENT

Rita sees herself as inferior to the 'proper' students but aspires to be like them. This shows her lack of confidence in the new environment, and also has much to do with her simply not understanding the realities of university education. As with her change of name, we recognise that in searching for her identity, she is simply moving further away from her true self. Her use of language is a barrier, the strong accent and **dialect** (see Literary Terms) clearly pitching her in the working class and setting her apart from the rest of the students. This, in turn, leads to a certain lack of confidence on Rita's part; something which she is only able to overcome in the second half of the play.

Willy Russell begins to develop the **theme** (see Literary Terms) of education through Rita's story of her schooldays, and the idea is picked up later when she

As Educating
Rita *develops, it*
becomes apparent
that both
characters are
learning from each
other.

relates how she once saw a beautiful bird as a child but refrained from telling the teacher because she knew that the teacher would 'Make us write an essay on it'. Frank acknowledges this, and the analogy (see Literary Terms) with the bird is related to Rita's own situation. He knows that for Rita to pass an examination in English Literature she must do more than simply admire the beauty of great works; she must also analyse them and communicate her ideas in writing.

Willy Russell's use of humour becomes more pronounced in this scene as the two characters begin to feed off each other. Rita's rather coarse and vulgar humour is countered by Frank's dry wit and the two contrasting styles work well together.

GLOSSARY   patina used here, it refers to Frank's room where the untidiness reflects his character

Tracy Austin a young American tennis star who shot to prominence in the 1980s

F.R. Leavis a popular twentieth-century literary critic

Marxist viewpoint Marxists analyse literature by looking at texts in the context of events occurring in society at the time of writing, just as Rita does with *Howards End*

SCENE 3   Rita is struggling to come to terms with E.M. Forster's novel *Howards End*. She pronounces, 'This Forster, honest to God he doesn't half get on my tits' to which Frank replies, 'Good. You must show me the evidence'. This quick-witted reply reflects the closeness that is developing in their relationship.

When Frank asks Rita to compare *Howards End* to two other novels she has read that week, her reply depicts the difficulties she is finding in the traditional learning process.

Rita's essay on Forster refers almost entirely to the popular novelist Harold Robbins, and Frank is unimpressed. He stresses the need for her to develop taste in literature for, if she fails to appreciate anything other than pulp fiction, she will never be prepared for the examination. The final part of the scene suggests that Rita is finally getting the message when she admits 'My mind's full of junk' and 'It needs a good clearin' out'.

COMMENT   Willy Russell said that this scene could be omitted when performing the play because it is not strictly essential in terms of the development of the **plot** (see Literary Terms). It is worth considering, however, what the play would lose by its omission.

Frank's attitude towards Rita and her education, after his early indifference, is very positive. A bond is emerging between the two characters and their relationship benefits them both. Rita receives the education which she craves and Frank, for his part, is given a new lease of life by Rita's exuberant enthusiasm.

Consider what effect Denny's lack of support for Rita's education has on their marriage.

When Rita confesses that the past week has been 'dead quiet in the shop' so she has been able to read three novels, it prepares us for her later admission that she writes her essays there too. This is the first indication that all is not well with her marriage to Denny and, more particularly, that he is not supporting her in her studies.

In trying to understand Frank's comment that she can continue to read her racy novels as long as she doesn't write about them in the examination, Rita has to put the concept into her own language before she fully grasps his meaning: 'You mean, it's all right to go out an' have a bit of slap an' tickle with the lads as long as you don't go home an' tell your mum?' Throughout the rest of the play, Rita's intellectual development goes hand-in-hand with the development of her language.

The openings and endings of the scenes are usually
dramatic, humorous, or both. Willy Russell is acutely
aware of the need to grab the attention of the audience
at the outset and then end on a powerful note, as if to
carry over the momentum into the next scene. The end
of this scene marks an important shift in attitude for
Rita. Her admission that her mind is full of 'junk' and
requires 'clearin' out' is evidence of a growing self-
awareness.

GLOSSARY   **Sons and Lovers** a novel by D.H. Lawrence (1885–1936)

SCENE 4   When Rita comes on stage at the beginning of this
scene, it is in stark contrast to her earlier entrances. As
she walks in the room, she shuts the door and stands
still, an unusual action considering her animated
movements of the previous scenes. As she wrestles with
her studies, in this case Forster's novel, her whole
character begins to change and develop. Her mind
freezes when contemplating Forster's phrase, 'only
connect', which has her completely baffled. For the
moment, however, Frank is more concerned with Rita's
one-line response to an essay on Ibsen's *Peer Gynt*. It is
now that we learn that Rita, unsupported by her
husband, does all her studying in the shop. Because the
salon has been so busy during the week, Rita has been
forced to encapsulate all her ideas into the briefest of
responses.

Frank tells Rita that, in an examination, there is a
certain way of answering questions that is expected and,
if she is to pass, then she must conform. So, to allow
her the opportunity of succeeding, he sets aside some
time during the tutorial for Rita to write a more
considered answer.

Rita possesses a   Sparked off by the thought of Peer Gynt's search for
negative vision of   the meaning of life, Rita digresses about one of her
the working-class   customers who wished to do the same thing. She also
culture.

adds that such a feeling is common to the working class, who appear to have lost their 'culture'. All she sees is 'everyone pissed, or on the Valium, tryin' to get from one day to the next'. She likens it to a disease which no one dare mention and draws parallels with events in her own marriage. In identifying all these links, Frank points out that she is doing exactly what Forster was suggesting when he advised, 'only connect'.

This is a valuable lesson for Rita and, along with the subsequent reasonable success of her *Peer Gynt* essay (at least, compared to her first attempt!), it strengthens the notion that, very gradually, she is becoming a 'proper' student.

COMMENT   Just as Rita conformed to expectations at school by not trying to succeed, she now has to conform to the expectations of examiners by adapting her style of language.

The conflict between home and studying becomes more apparent in this scene. Perhaps Denny realises that education will take Rita away from him. If so, it is **ironic** (see Literary Terms) that, in not supporting his wife's studies, he creates an even bigger division between the two of them.

Note how Rita is becoming increasingly conscious of her own use of language.

Rita is being moulded and changed by Frank. Her character undergoes a major transformation, even to the extent of altering her natural speech. The language of the essay is not Rita's. Rather, it is the voice of a 'proper' student and, when we witness her success with the essay, we recognise that Rita is well on the way towards her ultimate goal.

GLOSSARY

Peer Gynt a play by Norwegian dramatist, Henrik Ibsen (1828–1906)

Valium a tranquillising drug

the Unions trade unions which are bodies of workers set up to improve working conditions

A *Identify the writers Rita is talking about.*

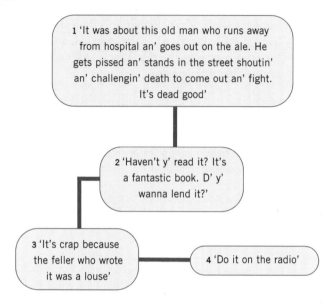

1 'It was about this old man who runs away from hospital an' goes out on the ale. He gets pissed an' stands in the street shoutin' an' challengin' death to come out an' fight. It's dead good'

2 'Haven't y' read it? It's a fantastic book. D' y' wanna lend it?'

3 'It's crap because the feller who wrote it was a louse'

4 'Do it on the radio'

Check your answers on page 67.

 B *Consider these issues.*

a The effect Rita's entrances have on the audience.

b Why Frank describes Rita as 'the first breath of air that's been in this room for years'.

c Why Frank tries to persuade Rita to opt for another tutor.

d The reasons for Frank's drink problems.

e Why Rita was unsuccessful at school.

f The problems faced by Rita in restarting her education as an adult.

g The reasons for changing her name from Susan to Rita.

h What Rita feels about working-class 'culture'.

ACT I   (CONTINUED)

SCENE 5

Do you think it is inevitable that the marriage will break down?

Rita's problems at home are intensified when we learn that Denny has burned all her books after finding that she was taking contraceptive pills again. She states that it is as if she was having an affair, although all she is doing is 'findin' meself'. Rita recognises that this is the root of her marital crisis. She has changed and left Denny 'wonderin' where the girl he married has gone to'.

The audience senses that the turning point for Rita is when Frank asks her whether she wants to discontinue the course. There is no hesitation in her reply, 'No. No!' and rather than discussing her marriage problems, it is significant that Rita chooses to talk about Chekhov instead. It is literature, she claims, which gives her life.

When he searches for the play on the top shelf, Frank discovers a bottle of whisky which he brings down and pours for himself and Rita. His drink problem is known about by his employers, but, Frank says, they turn a blind eye to it so long as Frank is discreet and takes care to hide the signs. His drinking has become heavier since he ceased writing poetry, and when he is pressed by Rita, he confides that he stopped because he 'got it wrong'. Instead of creating poetry, he was trying to create literature. The scene ends with Rita persuading Frank to visit an amateur production of *The Importance of Being Earnest*.

COMMENT

Like Frank's poetry, Rita's analysis of literature is cold and detached.

Frank admits that he stopped writing poetry because of a lack of inspiration, but he is also critical of his poetic style. His poetry was so finely crafted and academic in its style that it was almost devoid of real life. Because he has spent all his life in university circles, mixing with academics all the time, his writing became rather dry and intellectual.

There is a clear parallel to be drawn between Frank's criticism of his own poetry and the way he is attempting to educate Rita. Just as his poetry is emotionally barren, so he is pushing Rita in the same direction. The more educated she becomes, the less flamboyant is her language and behaviour. Instead of responding to texts naturally and with honesty from the heart, she learns to use her mind to analyse them in a rather cold and characterless fashion. It would appear that to succeed in the academic world, it is necessary for Rita to curb her lively ways and be transformed into a 'proper' student.

GLOSSARY   **The Seagull** a play by Anton Chekhov (1860–1904)

                 The Importance of Bein' Thingy *The Importance of Being Earnest,* a play by Oscar Wilde (1854–1900)

SCENE 6

Rita now chooses to spend her evenings at the theatre rather than in the pub.

Frank's moment of relaxation at the beginning of this scene is quickly shattered when Rita bursts through the door in a state of intense excitement, after visiting a professional theatre the night before. She is desperate to talk about the play, *Macbeth*, but finds it difficult to express her ideas: 'Wasn't his wife a cow, eh?'

Frank discusses the concept of tragedy (see Literary Terms) with Rita, as opposed to something which is tragic. Rita invites Frank to an art gallery the next day and the scene ends with Frank's invitation to Rita to attend a dinner party organised by his partner, Julia. Denny is also invited but Rita suspects that he will not go. Her lack of confidence is expressed by her final question, 'What shall I wear?'

COMMENT

If the audience had begun to accept that Rita was well on the route to academic success, then they are allowed to see her limitations at first-hand when she discusses *Macbeth* with Frank.

Rita's lack of a critical, academic vocabulary is not her only limitation at this time. In terms of literary concepts, she demonstrates her lack of knowledge when discussing the notion of tragedy. Rita responds to literature from the heart. Whereas Frank is critical and detached, Rita becomes involved and engaged with the characters on stage, almost to the point of shouting out loud to warn Macbeth of his impending doom.

Throughout the play, however, Rita demonstrates a certain amount of self-awareness. Looking out of the window, she sees the other students who she is desperately trying to emulate and recognises that she is not yet one of them.

Think about the balance between humour and seriousness in the play.

There is a constant thread of humour running throughout the play. Note how Rita's language is, once again, the source of much comedy in the play. When she suddenly remembers that she should have been back at work a long time ago, her reaction is typical: 'Christ – me customer. She only wanted a demi-wave – she'll come out looking like a friggin' muppet.'

Rita's lack of confidence to Frank's invitation has links with the next scene where we find that Rita has been unable to attend the party through fear of making a fool of herself, whether it be to do with wearing the wrong clothes, saying the wrong things or even taking the wrong wine. Her metamorphosis into a confident, educated woman is far from complete.

GLOSSARY **Pre-ordained** written in the stars, decided previously

SCENE 7 This is a pivotal scene in Rita's development. Having been unable to pluck up the confidence or courage to cross over the threshold at Frank's dinner party, she now comes to explain why. One of Rita's concerns was that she might have brought the wrong type of wine. Here again, Willy Russell undercuts the seriousness of

the situation with his humour. 'It wouldn't have
mattered if you'd walked in with a bottle of Spanish
plonk' says Frank. 'It was Spanish' comes the reply.

Frank asks Rita why she simply couldn't be herself, and
she admits that it's because she doesn't want to be
'myself'. She wants to become a different person, but at
this stage of the play she is trapped between two
worlds, a 'half-caste' as she describes herself. She is
uncomfortable with the people she lives with and yet
does not fit in with Frank's world either.

The reaction of
Rita's mother
strengthens her
convictions.

Initially, her reaction was to stop visiting Frank's
tutorials and get on with her life. However, on going
back to the pub where her family are enjoying a
Saturday night sing-song, she sees her mother crying.
When she asks her why, her mother replies 'because
we could sing better songs than those'. Rita recognises
the significance of this comment immediately. Just like
her mother, Rita is **metaphorically** (see Literary
Terms) searching for a new 'song' to sing, and that is
why she eventually decides to carry on with her
education.

COMMENT

The invitation to dinner is partly a **symbolic** (see
Literary Terms) act. To attend the function would
signify acceptance in Frank's social circle, and yet Rita
knows that she is not ready for the transition from her
world into that of Frank. She fails to do it at this stage
because she knows in her heart that she does not
possess the language, the knowledge or the style of the
middle-class academics to whom she aspires.

It is interesting to note that Frank describes Rita's
character as 'funny, delightful, charming' but Rita,
herself, rejects his attempts to compliment her as being
patronising. She does not want to be funny but wants
to 'talk seriously with the rest of you'. Spurred on by
this desire, Rita's metamorphosis gathers momentum.

For the people in Rita's family, Saturday night is spent at the local pub. The play sets up the contrast between this working-class culture as opposed to the culture of the middle class, who are seen to entertain themselves at dinner parties or at the theatre.

The act of Rita's mother crying has a **metaphorical** (see Literary Terms) significance. Denny gets her laughing again and, because we have made the connection between Rita and her mother who are both dissatisfied with their lives, we are forced to consider the logical argument that the same could happen to Rita. The laughter could very easily cover the pain which exists just below the surface.

GLOSSARY   Shaw   George Bernard Shaw (1856–1950), an Irish dramatist

SCENE 8   Rita tells Frank how Denny has given her the ultimatum: either stop studying and come off the pill or leave altogether. Having chosen the latter, she turns up at Frank's room with her suitcase. Rita has arranged to spend some time with her mother until she can find a flat of her own.

Note how Rita uses the end of her marriage to spur her on to succeed with her studies.

Under the circumstances, Frank is finding it difficult to carry on 'business as usual' and is reticent about criticising one of Rita's essays. Yet Rita wants to discuss her *Macbeth* essay, rather than dwelling on her home troubles with Denny, in a similar way that she wanted to talk about Chekhov and Frank tried to get her to forget studies and focus on what was happening in her life in Scene 5. Frank therefore discusses Rita's essay, telling her that it is 'totally honest' and 'moving', but in terms of helping her pass exams it is 'worthless'. Rita asks how to go about changing this, but Frank states he does not know if he can do this as he will have to change her. However, Rita is adamant that

she wants to change and she needs Frank to help in
her education, even if it means abandoning her
'uniqueness'.

Rita's strength and determination shine through when,
at the end of the scene, the curtain closes with her
tearing up the essay, dumping it in the bin and
preparing to 'start again'.

COMMENT

*In attempting to
change, Rita is
leaving her family
and friends
behind.*

Note how Rita's changing character is causing her to
leave 'Susan' further and further behind. The
dissolution of her marriage is the last tie with her
former life and Rita is now free to develop as she
pleases. Any sadness or sympathy we feel for Denny
disappears when we consider the way he has restricted
her intellectual growth. In addition, there is also the
notion that he, too, is a free agent once again and that
he will, undoubtedly find another wife, and probably
someone who is more suited to his lifestyle and his
desire for children.

*Frank is concerned
that Rita's
development might
not, necessarily, be
entirely for the best.*

When Frank tells Rita that, for her to succeed, she
may have to abandon her 'uniqueness', he is recognising
that to change Rita's entire being may not necessarily
be a wholly positive achievement. Having witnessed the
destruction of her marriage as a direct result of her
education, he is rightly concerned that, instead of

finding herself, she may in fact be losing her true identity. Furthermore, it is apparent to Frank that in training Rita to quell her vibrant character and write from the head rather than the heart, he is actually negating all those features which attracted him to Rita in the first place.

This is a crucial scene which encapsulates Rita's personality, aims and desires, and is a highly dramatic way of bringing this first act to an end. Rita's determination to change prepares us for Act II.

GLOSSARY   narked a slang expression for annoyed

A *Identify the people Rita and Frank are talking about.*

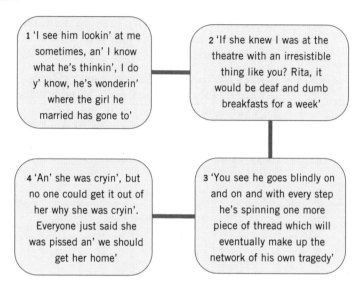

1 'I see him lookin' at me sometimes, an' I know what he's thinkin', I do y' know, he's wonderin' where the girl he married has gone to'

2 'If she knew I was at the theatre with an irresistible thing like you? Rita, it would be deaf and dumb breakfasts for a week'

4 'An' she was cryin', but no one could get it out of her why she was cryin'. Everyone just said she was pissed an' we should get her home'

3 'You see he goes blindly on and on and with every step he's spinning one more piece of thread which will eventually make up the network of his own tragedy'

Check your answers on page 67.

 B *Consider these issues.*

a The ways in which Willy Russell brings out humour in the play.

b Why Denny burns Rita's books.

c The differences in Rita's and Frank's use of language.

d The reasons why Rita could not go to Frank's dinner party.

e The way Rita responds to seeing *Macbeth*, compared with Frank's comments.

f Why Rita describes herself as a 'half-caste'.

g What happens in the pub and why it is a turning point in Rita's development.

ACT II

SCENE 1

Compare Rita's entrance with her opening entrance of Act I.

A significant amount of time has elapsed since Act I. Frank has, once again, begun to write poetry and, when Rita enters, she is a different Rita, bursting through the door as usual but this time dressed in new second-hand clothes which she displays for Frank in the form of a twirl.

Rita's success at summer school means that she is brimming with confidence. She has stopped smoking, moved in with a new flatmate called Trish and, as she admits, 'I'm havin' the time of me life'.

Frank, on the other hand, is having a bad time of it. Julia has left him during the summer and, although she has now returned, Frank is still drinking heavily. Moreover, Rita's present of a pen with the inscription, 'Must only be used for poetry' only serves as a further reminder of his own creative failings. Rita is attempting to reform him, but Frank knows only too well that Rita's influence is a temporary measure and that, like all students, her leaving is inevitable.

To change the mood, Frank tries to introduce Rita to the work of a 'new' poet but he is surprised to learn that

For the first time, Frank realises that he is not fully in control of Rita's education.

she has already 'done' William Blake at summer school. Rita recites a poem from memory and explains that even though Blake was not on the syllabus, one of her tutors was such a 'Blake freak' that she ended up reading his works anyway.

COMMENT

Rita is curbing her 'uniqueness' and taking a serious attitude towards her studies.

Rita's changing language is instantly recognisable. When she tells Frank about her conversation with the tutor who asked her whether she was fond of Ferlinghetti, Rita acknowledges that the old Rita would have said 'only with Parmesan cheese'. Instead, her reply is a carefully controlled and serious response: 'Actually I'm not too familiar with the American poets.' She also uses words like **analogy**, **parody** and **tragedy** with apparent ease, in contrast to not knowing what **assonance** (see Literary Terms) meant at the beginning of Act I. Note, also, how she is beginning to echo the words of Trish, her flatmate, when stating that 'A room is like a plant'.

Frank is being stifled by his lecturer's role in the university. It offers little creativity and gives him no satisfaction. On top of this, his relationship with Julia seems to have stagnated. Rita senses this, wanting to throw open the windows and bring new life to Frank's room.

With Rita's newly acquired confidence and intellectual maturity, we detect a subtle shift in the balance of their relationship. Frank's relevance to Rita is not quite what it was at the beginning of her education. For example, her assertion that she had already 'done' Blake at summer school is the first occasion when Rita surprises Frank with her literary knowledge. Putting the book back on the shelf is significant, indicating that, for once, Frank has fallen out of step with Rita's education. The fact that she developed good relationships with other tutors on the course means the beginning of a sense of insecurity and even jealousy for Frank.

GLOSSARY   **Ferlinghetti** Lawrence Ferlinghetti, an American poet
                    Blake William Blake (1757–1827), an English poet, painter and engraver

SCENE *2*

Rita appears rather comical and foolish, taking things too far.

Arriving late for her tutorial, Rita begins by speaking with an affected voice which she sees as 'talking properly'. Her flatmate, Trish, has told her that 'there is not a lot of point in discussing beautiful literature in an ugly voice', but Frank is quick to point out that she hasn't got an ugly voice, or at least she didn't have. He tells her to be herself but, as Rita indicated earlier in the play she is trying to become educated simply to avoid being 'meself'.

Continuing from her success at the summer school and her growing confidence which has resulted in her changing character, we now learn that for the first time, Rita has actually mixed with the 'proper' students and she has quickly realised that they are not so infallible after all. Her illusions of their academic prowess are shattered as she wins her argument with the other students about D.H. Lawrence.

Note the element of discord which is creeping into the relationship of Frank and Rita.

Rita reports that one of the students, nicknamed Tiger, has invited her on a Christmas vacation to the south of France with the rest of his crowd. Frank reacts with what appears to be jealousy, making excuses about why she would be unable to go.

Rita is shocked and cuts Frank short, suggesting that he is being ridiculous. The scene ends, however, with Frank returning one of Rita's essays, telling her that it 'wouldn't look out of place' with the work of the other students on his desk.

COMMENT   Rita is late because she has been talking to the other
           students down on the grass and this represents a shift in
           her attitude and confidence. Rita is now able to hold
           her own in academic circles, whether it be down on the
           lawns below Frank's window or in a more formal
           manner at the summer school.

           Trish is becoming another influence in her life. She is a
           different form of teacher and becomes a sort of role
           model for Rita.

           Placing the essay on top of the pile is **symbolic** (see
           Literary Terms). Rita has finally 'made it'. No longer is
           she out of place, and no longer can she describe herself
           as a 'half-caste'.

GLOSSARY   **Dalek** referring to the popular sci-fi programme Dr Who, a robot
            with an electronic voice
            spoutin' a slang expression meaning talking at length
            Lady Chatterley **to** *Sons and Lovers* novels by the English writer
            D.H. Lawrence (1885–1930); the full title of *Lady Chatterley*
            is *Lady Chatterley's Lover*

SCENE 3   The lights come up on Rita, and it is Frank who is very
            drunk that makes the dramatic, if rather clumsy
Note the unusual   entrance. He has been reported by some students for
opening of this   being drunk and falling off the rostrum when delivering
scene.   a lecture. The university authorities have stopped short
            of giving Frank the sack, but he is being forced to take
            a sabbatical somewhere abroad for a year or so,
            presumably to get him out of the way.

            Frank reveals his feelings of discontent towards his
            regular students when describing them as 'a crowd of
            mealy-mouthed pricks who wouldn't know a poet if you
            beat them about the head with one'. In his lecture, he
            has quoted Rita's line from earlier in the play:
            'Assonance means getting the rhyme wrong'. Rather
            understandably, the students are disdainful for they do

not share Frank's understanding of the line. Out of context, it sounds ridiculous.

Frank's
reservations
about Rita's
development
come to the fore
in this scene.

Rita is ready to postpone the tutorial until the following week, but Frank engages her in a conversation about her essay on William Blake. He concedes that if it were written in an examination it would earn a high grade, but he dislikes it because it is too impersonal. Rita complains that, in the beginning, Frank had urged her to write in this objective style. The dialogue develops into an argument with Rita confirming that she no longer needs Frank as much as she used to when she first started attending his classes.

The scene ends on a lighter, if not **ironic** (see Literary Terms), note with Frank stating that he had read *Rubyfruit Jungle* and liked it, a book Rita had referred to in Act I Scene 1.

COMMENT Note how Frank is lapsing into Rita's language, using the phrase 'Completely off my cake'. He also swears at the start of the scene, uses her original definitions of literary terms like **assonance**, and is even reading the books she read, reminiscent of Rita at the beginning of the play.

By educating Rita, Frank changes her, but he also wants to retain the old Rita. The more she develops, the less she reminds him of the 'girl' who walked through his door and brought a 'breath of air' to his life. **Ironically** (see Literary Terms), this is akin to Denny's reaction in the first half of the play when he, too, wondered where the 'girl' he married had gone to.

The scene confirms that Rita does not need Frank as much as she needed him earlier in the play, and it is seemingly inevitable that their relationship will break down. Frank had always perceived that Rita would only need him for a short time before she was able to exist independently, but this does not lessen the blow for him. Once again, just like Denny who precipitated the marriage breakdown, Frank's petulant behaviour only serves to create further problems with Rita.

GLOSSARY   sabbatical paid leave from your place of employment
Australia might be more apt referring to the time when British criminals were transported to Australia

A *Identify the people Rita and Frank are talking about.*

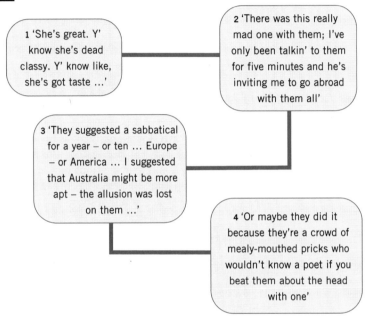

1 'She's great. Y' know she's dead classy. Y' know like, she's got taste ...'

2 'There was this really mad one with them; I've only been talkin' to them for five minutes and he's inviting me to go abroad with them all'

3 'They suggested a sabbatical for a year – or ten ... Europe – or America ... I suggested that Australia might be more apt – the allusion was lost on them ...'

4 'Or maybe they did it because they're a crowd of mealy-mouthed pricks who wouldn't know a poet if you beat them about the head with one'

Check your answers on page 67.

 B *Consider these issues.*

a The difference in Rita's character compared with before the interval.

b The punishment dealt out by the university authorities was unfair.

c Frank's reaction to the news that Rita has been invited to go to the south of France for Christmas with the other students.

d The influence which Trish has over Rita.

e Frank's surprise when finding out that Rita has already studied Blake's poetry.

f What Rita learns when she plucks up the courage to talk to the other students down on the grass.

g As Rita becomes more learned and more educated, Frank criticises her essays for not containing any of her own views.

ACT **II**   (CONTINUED)

SCENE **4**   Because Rita is late for her tutorial, Frank rings the hairdresser's shop only to find that she has left her job. She now works in a bistro. When questioning Rita about why she has done this, and why she hasn't told him, she says she is fed up of talking about 'irrelevant rubbish' and she is now able to talk 'about what's important'.

Frank asks whether Mr Tyson, or Tiger as he is known to his friends, is one of Rita's customers at the bistro. She admits that he is and that she finds him and the other students fascinating. She enjoys being in their company because they are so full of life.

Frank's reaction is to ask whether she can be bothered to attend the classes anymore and to suggest that she now dislikes spending any amount of time there. Rita's reply is emphatic: 'For God's sake, I don't want to stop coming here. I've got to come here. What about my exam?'

Throughout the scene, Frank is pouring whisky down his throat and Rita is blunt when telling him that if he stopped drinking, he 'might be able to talk about things that matter instead of where I do or don't work; an' then it might be worth comin' here'.

Would Frank have   In an attempt to test whether Rita does or does not
given Rita the   know what 'matters', Frank hands her some of his own
poems if he had not   poetry, asking for a critical, non-subjective and non-
been drinking?   sentimental appraisal by the following week.

COMMENT   The change in jobs is part of Rita's metamorphosis into an entirely different character. Just like changing her name and trying to alter the sound of her own voice, it reflects a desire to put her previous existence firmly in the past.

Frank's apparent jealousy over Tiger makes him seem insecure and almost like a schoolboy. The reason, presumably, is that Frank feels that he is 'losing' Rita. When he says, 'perhaps you don't want to waste your time coming here anymore?' he cuts a rather pathetic figure, wallowing in his own misery. Drink, however, clearly plays a part in this scene and accentuates Frank's reactions.

Asking Rita to criticise his poetry is Frank's idea of a 'test', not in the conventional sense, but in the sense that it will clarify whether or not Rita has lost the ability to respond openly and honestly. He is afraid that she has lost her 'uniqueness' and that she has become cold and subjective like the rest of his students whom he despises so much.

SCENE 5

Frank is testing Rita by giving her the poems to analyse.

Having sat up late with her flatmate, Trish, to read Frank's poems, Rita returns the following day to his room at the university, full of praise for his work. She describes the poems as 'brilliant', 'witty', 'profound' and 'full of style', but Frank's view is in stark contrast: 'this clever, pyrotechnical pile of self-conscious allusion is worthless, talentless shit and should be recognized as such by anyone with a shred of common sense.' He makes the point that Rita, when she first started her visits, would have said exactly the same. He feels that like Mary Shelley, writer of *Frankenstein*, he has created his own 'monster'. He recognises that the Rita who first brought that 'breath of air' into his room has gone forever. In describing the poems as 'pretentious, characterless and without style', he is suggesting that the new Rita who admires them so much must possess these same qualities.

Leaving the room after being insulted, Rita tells Frank that she no longer needs him because she is now educated with a 'room full of books'. She now knows 'what clothes to wear' and 'what wine to buy, what plays to see, what papers and books to read'. Frank sees this as worthless, that her newly found culture is no better than her past. He says that she has not found a 'better song' but a 'different song', which does not fit with who she is.

As she leaves, he calls her Rita and she laughs in his face. She says that no one calls her Rita any more but him and that she 'dropped' the name when she realised it was 'pretentious crap'.

COMMENT

Note the allusion to Act I Scene 7.

When Frank asks Rita, 'Found a culture have you Rita? Found a better song to sing have you?' he is referring to the night when Rita is in the pub and she spots her mother crying. The 'song' represents an alternative and better lifestyle. Frank, however, is not convinced that Rita has found anything better.

The relationship is clearly breaking down. Frank regrets the way Rita has altered and blames himself.

The change of name seals the metamorphosis of Rita's character. Instead of playing at being different, Rita has finally found her true self. She no longer needs to hide behind a new name and accepts that she is Susan. Frank's name-calling, unfortunately, suggests that he feels Rita has still not 'found herself'.

GLOSSARY

classical allusion references to the works of great writers from the past

Mary Shelley writer (1797–1851) of the Gothic novel, *Frankenstein*, which Frank refers to

Gothic eighteennth-century novels which deal with macabre or mysterious events, often in remote or desolate settings

Virginia ... Charlotte ... Jane ... Emily Frank refers to Virginia Woolf, Charlotte Brontë, Jane Austen and Emily Brontë, all British women novelists, in order to mock Rita

SCENE 6

This short scene begins with Frank's telephone call to the bistro in order to inform Rita that she has been entered for her examination.

Think about
Frank's reasons for
ringing Rita.

Initially, he asks for Rita but quickly realises his mistake and changes the name to Susan. As she is not there, he is forced to hang up. There is a black-out to denote the passing of time and when the lights come up again he is talking to Trish over the phone, giving her details of the examination to pass on to Rita. Here, again, he cannot become accustomed to calling her Susan: 'Erm, yes I'm a friend of Rita's ... Rita ... I'm sorry Susan.'

COMMENT

The telephone calls show that, since his last meeting with Rita, Frank has had time to consider his words and actions, and come to the realisation that Rita should at least have the opportunity of sitting her examination.

Frank is unable to accept the change of name because it represents the change in character. As she arrived with the name of Rita, Frank will always associate it with the 'breath of air' which swept into his room on the night of her first tutorial.

SCENE 7

Consider the effect
on the audience of
Frank packing his
belongings into the
tea-chests.

The final scene opens with Rita, smoking again and wearing a large winter coat to illustrate that time has, once again, moved on. It is now close to Christmas and Rita has passed her examination. She is returning to thank Frank for being a good teacher and is surprised to find him packing his belongings into several tea-chests.

The university authorities have been forced to respond to Frank's drink problem and, rather than sacking him, they are sending him away to Australia for two years. He tries to make light of it when joking that the Australians named their favourite drink after a literary figure: 'Forster's Lager they call it.' However, the laughter only just covers the pain he is undoubtedly going through. Julia is not going with him and this, effectively, means the end of their relationship.

Rita tells Frank about the question on *Peer Gynt* in her examination which was the same as the one set by Frank in one of her early tutorials. Earlier she simply wrote 'Do it on the radio' and Frank was critical. Now, she suspects that Frank would have been proud of her if she had responded in this way. It seems as though part of her wanted to, but she chose not to, and that ability to choose is the most important gift that Frank has been able to bestow on Rita. She also tells him about Trish, who was her model and teacher, trying to 'top' herself.

See how Frank's tentative suggestion that she should go to Australia with him reveals his lack of confidence.

Rita evades Frank's invitation to go to Australia and tells him that she's already been invited to the south of France with Tiger and his friends and to her mother's for Christmas. When Frank asks what she will do, she replies, 'I dunno. I might go to France. I might go to me mother's. I might even have a baby. I dunno. I'll make a decision. I'll choose.'

Frank gives Rita a present of a dress and Rita says that she feels that all she has ever done is to take things from Frank. However, there is one thing which she can do for him and, grabbing a pair of scissors from the desk, she prepares to cut his hair with the closing line, 'I'm gonna take ten years off you'.

COMMENT   Lighting a cigarette marks a partial return to Rita's old ways. In this scene we have evidence that Rita, or Susan as she is now known again, has matured into a confident and articulate woman who is finally at ease with herself. Even her language, although less rough around the edges, is more like her speech at the start of the play. No longer does she feel it necessary to change her voice, she can simply be herself.

When talking about 'Forster's Lager', Frank is referring to Rita's early error over the spelling of E.M. Forster's name. Note how this comes about in the form of gentle teasing. It is noticeable that the warmth and light-hearted way of talking has returned to their relationship.

The present of the dress refers to earlier in the play when Rita refused to buy a new dress until she passed her first examination. Frank's love for Rita, possibly suggested by his jealousy earlier in the play, now becomes evident as he shows that he has remembered her words and acted with tenderness in buying the gift.

Note how the comic framework of the play is re-established right at the end. The ending of the play has distinctly sexual overtones, when Rita suggests that there is one thing that she can do for him to say thank you for all his teaching. In a moment of comic genius, Willy Russell has Rita undercut the tension of the scene by taking out a pair of scissors to trim Frank's hair.

GLOSSARY   metaphorically see metaphor in Literary Terms

Forster's Lager a well-known brand of Australian lager, but Frank is jokingly referring to Rita's early confusion over the names when reading the work of E.M. Forster

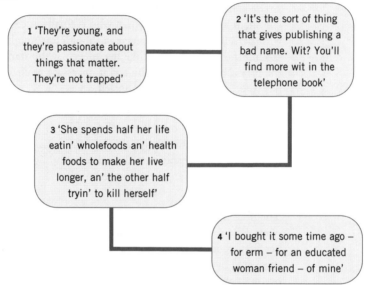

A *Identify the people referred to in these lines.*

1 'They're young, and they're passionate about things that matter. They're not trapped'

2 'It's the sort of thing that gives publishing a bad name. Wit? You'll find more wit in the telephone book'

3 'She spends half her life eatin' wholefoods an' health foods to make her live longer, an' the other half tryin' to kill herself'

4 'I bought it some time ago – for erm – for an educated woman friend – of mine'

Check your answers on page 67.

B *Consider these issues.*

a Why Rita neglects to tell Frank that she has left the hairdresser's and begun work in a bistro.

b Why Frank gives his poems to Rita.

c Rita's assessment of his poetry and Frank's reaction to it.

d Why she has reverted back to the name of Susan and why Frank still calls her Rita.

e What Rita feels that education has given her.

f The significance of Frank's present to Rita.

g Why the comic ending is so effective.

PART THREE

COMMENTARY

THEMES

PEOPLE AND ENVIRONMENT

Frank

With all the action taking place in Frank's study, we always see him in the middle of his own environment. The room is cluttered with books and his other belongings. Comfortable to the point of stagnation,

Consider how far both characters are forced to reassess their positions in society.

it is only when Rita comes on the scene that the room has its first 'breath of life' for many years. Later in the play, she feels the need to throw open the window saying that 'a room is like a plant' and it needs air. This stifling, rather oppressive atmosphere could be one reason for Frank's lack of creativity. Ironically (see Literary Terms), at the end of the play, the audience senses that his imminent banishment to Australia could be just the thing to spark off some form of poetic inspiration.

Rita

Quite the opposite to Frank, Rita is cast into an alien environment right from the beginning and, initially, she appears to be like a fish out of water. Her accent

As with many of Willy Russell's plays, the 'class' issue is never far from the surface.

and dialect (see Literary Terms) compared with Frank's assured use of 'Standard English', and her working-class, non-academic background clearly set her apart from Frank's 'proper' students. The resultant lack of confidence causes Rita to baulk at going to Frank's dinner party because she knows that she doesn't fit in. Sadly, she also realises that, having outgrown her family and friends, she no longer belongs in her own class either. Describing herself as a 'freak' and a 'half-caste' who is stuck between two worlds, she realises that she must either turn the clock back and return to her former life, or press ahead with her education and become accepted in a new

environment – the social circles inhabited by the other
university students.

INCOMPLETENESS

In terms of their characters, both Frank and Rita show
an alarming sense of incompleteness.

Rita

Rita, in particular, is driven by the need for education,
having realised that life has more to offer than her
mundane existence in a hairdressing salon. At the age
of twenty-six she feels 'out of step' and tells Frank that,
before considering having a baby with Denny, she
would need to discover herself first. Ultimately, this
costs Rita her marriage, her friends and her job.

Although Frank suggests that her education results
merely in her 'singing a different song', rather than
achieving a necessarily better life, the Rita at the end of
the play is a whole, rounded character, who possesses
the knowledge, skills and confidence to choose her own
direction in life.

Frank

Frank, too, has something lacking in his life. His rather
jaded outlook not only results in poor teaching for the
majority of his students, but it also blocks his poetic

Instead of creativity. Already divorced from his wife, his
considering Frank's relationship with Julia does not appear set to last and he
banishment as a seeks comfort from all his problems in the form of a
punishment, how whisky bottle. Unlike Rita, he fails to attain a sense of
easy is it to view completeness in the play. However, the prospect of a
his trip to Australia new life in Australia, where things are 'just beginning'
as a liberation? does at least offer some hope for the future.

Rita's family

Just like Frank, Rita's family all seek to escape from
their problems through alcohol. The Saturday night
sing-song in the local pub is suggestive of happiness
and family unity, but the reality of the situation is very
different. Their laughter and song is a thin veil which

covers up the painful knowledge that their lives are
unfulfilled and incomplete. Rita's mother shows that
she has achieved this state of self-knowledge when she
cries, saying that they could all be singing 'better songs
than those'.

METAMORPHOSIS

Rita's education is much more than simply learning
about English Literature. It represents a complete
change in her being. As Frank tells Rita, for her to pass
the examination, she must suppress or even abandon
her 'uniqueness'. 'I'm going to have to change you', he
says. Her lively, irrepressible nature is suppressed and
even her language undergoes a transformation, causing
Frank finally to regret the way he has changed her. In
doing so, he compares himself to Mary Shelley, the
author of *Frankenstein*, because he also feels that he has
created a 'monster'.

The metamorphosis is a slow and painful process for
Rita. Halfway through, she likens herself to a 'half-
caste', who is both out of place in her own society and
yet unable to fit into Frank's social circles too. The
change of name from Susan to Rita is significant, but in

What 'mistakes' attempting to create a new identity, Rita inevitably
does Rita make on makes mistakes. She is taken in by the vitality of Tiger
her journey to and the other students and treats her flatmate, Trish,
education? with reverence. However, by the end of the play, Rita
has seen the truth. Trish, having survived a suicide
attempt, is seen as neurotic and fragile, while Tiger is
simply 'a bit of a wanker really'. And, as if to seal the
change and acceptance of her character, she reverts back
to her original name.

Thus, Rita emerges from her metamorphosis as a
whole, more rounded character. Gone is the affected
language, and along with the return of her natural

speech comes the re-establishing of her vibrant sense
of humour. She has matured and, **symbolically**
(see Literary Terms), Frank's present of the dress
serves to emphasis this fact.

EDUCATION

Rita finds herself on an Open University course as a
direct result of her failure at school where studying was
'just for whimps'. She acknowledges that if she had
taken school seriously, she would have become different
to her friends.

Having broken free, to some extent, from that kind of
peer pressure, Rita's second attempt at education shows
her to be an enthusiastic and highly motivated student.
She has an idealised vision of 'proper' students, to
which she feels she does not belong. Frank's description
of his students is in stark contrast. 'Proper students
don't read and study', he tells Rita. They are 'appalling'
scholars who 'wouldn't know a poet if you beat them
about the head with one'.

Think about
Frank's strengths
and weaknesses as
a teacher.

Because her desire to change her direction in life sets
her apart from the other students, Frank is placed under
pressure. Rita wants to learn 'everything' and Frank
appears to baulk at the challenge. For the majority of
the time, his 'appalling teaching', as he describes it, is
'quite in order for most of my appalling students', but
Frank knows that Rita deserves better. Rita declines his
offer to find another tutor, sensing that their
compatibility will be all-important, and it is the
strength of their relationship which enables Rita to
develop into an excellent student.

What does Rita
gain from her
education and
what does she lose?

For Rita, education is a way out of an unfulfilling
lifestyle. In the final scene, after she has passed her
examination, she recognises that it may well have all
been worthless in the end, meaning that it may not

radically alter her life, but at least she now has some
element of choice in her life. She does not mean the
type of choices open to her husband, Denny, such as
choosing between the eight different kinds of lager in
the pub, but real choices which can affect the direction
of her life. She has the opportunity to make a fresh start
in Australia with Frank, she could carry on working in
the bistro, she could return to her old job as a
hairdresser, or she could choose to do something
completely different.

STRUCTURE

The play is **structured** (see Literary Terms) in two acts
and is perfectly balanced. The first half deals with Rita's
struggle to fit into Frank's world. He is the one who is
seen to be in control. He possesses all the knowledge
and speaks the right words. Rita, on the other hand, is
exactly the opposite in the sense that she struggles with
language in the beginning, only developing the
necessary skills to succeed in Act II, after her success at
the summer school.

Consider how far Just as the first half of the play sees the breakdown of
Frank's attitude is Rita's marriage, the second half contains evidence of a
responsible for the rift between Frank and Julia. Act I witnesses Rita's
conflict with Rita. gradual development to the point where she fits in,
whereas Act II reflects Frank's growing alienation from
the world of the academics, eventually resulting in his
banishment to Australia. The great **antithesis** (see
Literary Terms) in the play is the fact that the more
Rita is educated, the less she needs Frank, and the more
this leads to a relationship of conflict.

The interval is a 'hinge'. After the interval and her
success on the summer school course, Rita seems to be
a changed character. Rita now appears to be the one

beginning to take charge of the proceedings, and
Frank's attempts to select a poet for study backfires on
him, when Rita announces that she has already analysed
Blake's poetry on her summer course. Frank becomes
the character who is having problems, while Rita goes
from strength to strength.

The concluding scenes of the play reflect the increasing
sense of pace. They become shorter and there is the
undoubted feeling that time has elapsed in the build up
towards Rita's examination.

The play is **naturalistic** in its **setting** (see Literary
Terms). The one set allows all the action to take place
inside Frank's room and, by adhering to the **unity**
(see Literary Terms) of place, Willy Russell is able to
concentrate both on the drama and the humour of the
play.

CHARACTERS

RITA

Initially, Rita is out of place in the middle-class world
of the academics. Her language is coarse and vulgar,
and she does not possess the vocabulary to express
literary concepts on anything other than a basic level.
When she passes on the opportunity of attending
Frank's dinner party, she does so because she knows
that she will feel out of place in those surroundings.
She is preoccupied by wearing the right clothes and by
taking the correct type of wine, as well as worrying
about saying the right things.

As a student, Rita does not possess the self-confidence
of those people who attend his regular lectures.
Failure at school the first time round has meant that
Rita has developed an idealised vision of university

At first:
Common
Uneducated
Humorous

Finally:
Confident
Mature
Humorous

Is it inevitable
that Rita's
marriage will
break down?

education. She does not want to go down on the lawn below Frank's window because she feels inferior.

Almost inevitably, the first half of the play charts the problems encountered by Rita in her married life with Denny. Her education, it seems, takes her away from her family and friends into an entirely new sphere of life. Her husband wants her to have children and yet Rita knows that before she has a baby, she needs to get to know herself. She deceives Denny by taking the contraceptive pill against his will, and knows how the disintegration of their relationship is affecting him. In return, Denny's refusal to support Rita in her education not only causes problems for her, but it probably hastens the demise of their marriage. Rita has to study in quiet moments at work and, at one point in the play, we learn that in a fit of temper after finding that Rita is still taking contraceptives, Denny actually burns some of her books.

Rita's mother is an interesting character in as much as, like Rita, she perceives that there is more to life than is being offered to them at present. When she is crying in the pub, she says it is 'because we could sing better songs than those'. Rita uses this **metaphor** (see Literary Terms) to stiffen her resolve and work even harder at her education – for it seems the only way out.

Rita, herself, has a vision of the working class which is not entirely favourable. She is dismissive of the working-class culture and states that people are 'either pissed or on the Valium', simply trying to get by. This is what Rita is trying to avoid.

Throughout the play, it is clearly Frank who plays the largest role in 'educating' Rita. However, as the play develops, Rita begins to have other influences in her life. New tutors at summer school introduce her to some of the great poets and Trish, Rita's flatmate, provides a different sort of role model. Once she has overcome her feelings of inferiority towards the other students, Rita is introduced to a whole new peer group. She is no longer afraid to mix with them on the lawns, and her job in the bistro offers even wider social access to their circles.

Note the importance of the summer school in giving Rita confidence.

In the second half of the play, Rita changes quite dramatically as a character. She becomes more confident and takes control of situations herself. Her language changes and she learns to express herself effectively. Her dress sense also undergoes a change as she tries to find her true identity. The change of name from Rita back to Susan is also important in this search. It would be fair to say that, to some extent, Rita does lose herself in this section of the play. The way she changes her voice on the suggestion of Trish is one clear example of a woman who is searching for an identity. However, by the end of the play, Rita has emerged as a confident, articulate character who is perfectly at ease with herself.

FRANK

Tired

Frustrated

In need of change

In the opening scenes the audience receive a rather negative picture of Frank. His drinking is clearly becoming a problem and the reasons for this escapism are deeply ingrained. He is dissatisfied with his role in life. A previous marriage has failed and we soon learn that his present relationship is far from ideal. He is disrespectful towards his students and resents having to use valuable drinking time in the pub on mature students like Rita who have signed up for the Open University course. However, it is his recent inability to write poetry which creates most frustration in Frank.

Frank is the 'teacher' in the play, but what does he learn from Rita?

Rita gives Frank a new lease of life. The windows in his room are stuck fast, and even the door seems reluctant to allow free access. Frank welcomes the way Rita seems to shake him out of his lethargy. Later in the play she tells him that a room is like a plant and that he should open the windows, sensing perhaps that Frank needs change. Rita's personality is refreshing because she is so different to the other students. Her language, although frequently inappropriate for academic circles, is colourful and by contrast, Frank appears rather dull and lifeless: 'Tragedy in dramatic terms is inevitable, pre-ordained.' The impression the reader receives is that Frank has said this line too many times for it to mean anything to him. Just like Rita, he needs to rediscover himself.

Ironically (see Literary Terms), the more Rita develops, the less she needs Frank and so his self-esteem deteriorates. He eventually descends into shameful drunkenness, falling off the stage in the middle of his lecture. For Frank, witnessing Rita's development is not always a pleasurable experience. He is uneasy about her metamorphosis and is particularly concerned that, for Rita to be successful in her studies, she may have to abandon what he describes as her 'uniqueness'.

Despite the rift with Rita, the ending re-establishes the bond between the two characters. Frank tries to contact Rita about the examination, which demonstrates a genuine care and concern. Furthermore, the present of the dress serves to underline the tenderness and affection with which Frank regards Rita.

MINOR CHARACTERS

Although Frank and Rita are the only two figures to appear on stage, we are introduced to a number of other characters through their words. These minor characters have a significant part to play in the shaping of events in *Educating Rita* and their relevance needs to be emphasised.

Denny   Rita's husband fails to support her attempts to educate herself, which he sees as a threat. He wants her to have children and resents the fact that she does not share his desire.

Julia   Frank's partner is one of his ex-students. After the break-up of his marriage, Frank begins to live with Julia, but even from the beginning of the play it appears that their relationship is rather strained.

Rita's mother   Like Rita, she senses that there must be more to life than her present, mundane existence and is saddened by the feeling that she has wasted her opportunities of fulfilment. Unless Rita acts in a positive manner and changes her lifestyle, the audience suspects that this is how she, too, will end up.

Trish   Rita's flatmate. Following the breakdown of Rita's marriage, Trish becomes a type of role model for Rita, who is desperate to change, and Rita almost idolises her new friend. Only at the end of the play does Rita see Trish for what she really is, when her attempted suicide reflects that she, too, has her own problems and weaknesses.

Tiger   Tiger, so-called because of his surname 'Tyson', seems to be a leading figure among the students. He is a potential love interest for Rita, and Frank certainly appears to be jealous of him when he invites Rita to go to France with his group of friends.

Much of the play's humour is derived from Rita's style of talking and the contrast in speech between Frank and Rita. Rita's accent and **dialect** (see Literary Terms) clearly pitches her in the working class and clashes with Frank's middle-class academic language. The way she talks about the performance of *Macbeth* reflects her enthusiasm: 'But listen, it wasn't borin', it was bleedin' great.' Frank on the other hand, uses carefully measured tones: 'Tragedy in dramatic terms is inevitable, pre-ordained.' His vocabulary is rather jaded and lethargic, as though he has made this speech countless times before. The **irony** (see Literary Terms) of this exchange is that, although Rita does not possess the vocabulary to fully articulate her thoughts, the ideas that she does express are clearly on the right lines. Describing Lady Macbeth as 'a cow' and **assonance** (see Literary Terms) as 'getting the rhyme wrong' may, at first, seem laughable and inappropriate, but on reflection they are seen to be Rita's early attempts to find a suitable voice to express literary concepts and are refreshing in contrast to a typical academic response. Indeed, it is Rita's vibrant language which helps to enthuse Frank away from his unmotivated position.

Note how the development of language is inextricably linked with Rita's change in character.

In the second half of the play, Rita attempts to change her speech when Trish, her flatmate, advises that 'beautiful literature' should not be discussed in an 'ugly voice'. However, what Rita fails to realise is that her language is inextricably linked with her personality. Noticeably, at the end of the play when Rita is confident in the knowledge that she has passed the examination, her natural speech returns. Having rejected the false name of Rita in favour of her original name, Susan, she also rejects all the falseness of her affected speech.

In the same way that Rita's language changes, Frank picks up several of her phrases such as 'completely off my cake' and even resorts to swearing in the same style as Rita did at the beginning of the play.

Rita's coarseness, in itself, is humorous because it is so inappropriate: 'God, I've had enough of this. It's borin', that's what it is, bloody borin'. This Forster, honest to God he doesn't half get on my tits.' Frank's dry response of 'Good. You must show me the evidence' adds to the humour. This verbal sparring is between two completely different characters, coming from wildly contrasting backgrounds. Culture and language clash head on.

Look at the way Willy Russell controls the humour of the ending. The ending of the play is cleverly controlled by Willy Russell. When Rita tells Frank that there is just one thing left that she can do for him in order to say thank you for his teaching, the audience detects more than a hint of a sexual undertone. The comic ending is achieved when the tension of the final scene is alleviated by Rita taking out a pair of scissors and preparing to cut Frank's hair.

The style of the play is essentially **naturalistic** (see Literary Terms). The only characters to appear on stage are Frank and Rita while others, such as Denny and Julia, are introduced to the audience through the spoken word. The fact that the whole play is centred in Frank's room at the university also helps to establish the naturalistic feel of *Educating Rita*. By adhering to the **unity** (see Literary Terms) of place, Willy Russell is able to concentrate the audience's attention on the two central characters. He is able to highlight Rita's attempts to fit into this alien environment and reflect on the way Frank is prevented from stagnation by the 'breath of air' she brings with her.

PART FOUR

STUDY SKILLS

HOW TO USE QUOTATIONS

One of the secrets of success in writing essays is the way you use quotations. There are five basic principles:

- Put inverted commas at the beginning and end of the quotation
- Write the quotation exactly as it appears in the original
- Do not use a quotation that repeats what you have just written
- Use the quotation so that it fits into your sentence
- Keep the quotation as short as possible

Quotations should be used to develop the line of thought in your essays.

Your comment should not duplicate what is in your quotation. For example:

> Rita tells Frank that she couldn't go to the dinner party because she had bought the wrong sort of wine 'I couldn't. I'd bought the wrong sort of wine.'

Far more effective is to write:

> Rita explains to Frank that she couldn't go to the dinner party because she'd 'bought the wrong sort of wine'.

Quotations should be used to illustrate points:

> Near the end of the play, Frank's refers to Rita's decision to buy a new dress only after passing her exam: 'It's erm – well, it's er – it's a dress really. I bought it some time ago for erm – for an educated woman friend – of mine ...'

However, the most sophisticated way of using the writer's words is to embed them into your sentence:

> Rita's emotive appraisal of Macbeth as 'bleedin' great' reflects a freshness of approach that is entirely lacking in Frank's rather stilted language.

When you use quotations in this way, you are demonstrating the ability to use text as evidence to support your ideas - not simply including words from the original to prove you have read it.

Everyone writes differently. Work through the suggestions given here and adapt the advice to suit your own style and interests. This will improve your essay-writing skills and allow your personal voice to emerge.

The following points indicate in ascending order the skills of essay writing:

- Picking out one or two facts about the story and adding the odd detail
- Writing about the text by retelling the story
- Retelling the story and adding a quotation here and there
- Organising an answer which explains what is happening in the text and giving quotations to support what you write

....

- Writing in such a way as to show that you have thought about the intentions of the writer of the text and that you understand the techniques used
- Writing at some length, giving your viewpoint on the text and commenting by picking out details to support your views
- Looking at the text as a work of art, demonstrating clear critical judgement and explaining to the reader of your essay how the enjoyment of the text is assisted by literary devices, linguistic effects and psychological insights; showing how the text relates to the time when it was written

The dotted line above represents the division between lower and higher level grades. Higher-level performance begins when you start to consider your response as a reader of the text. The highest level is reached when you offer an enthusiastic personal response and show how this piece of literature is a product of its time.

*Coursework
essay*

Set aside an hour or so at the start of your work to plan what you have to do.

- List all the points you feel are needed to cover the task. Collect page references of information and quotations that will support what you have to say. A helpful tool is the highlighter pen: this saves painstaking copying and enables you to target precisely what you want to use.
- Focus on what you consider to be the main points of the essay. Try to sum up your argument in a single sentence, which could be the closing sentence of your essay. Depending on the essay title, it could be a statement about a character: Rita's changing character is reflected in her different ways of speaking, and her partial return to her original accent and dialect suggests a newly acquired confidence within herself; an opinion about setting: Frank's cluttered office reflects his own feelings of chaos and despair; or a judgement on a theme: I think that, although the title of the play is 'Educating Rita', it is obvious that Frank learns a lot too.
- Make a short essay plan. Use the first paragraph to introduce the argument you wish to make. In the following paragraphs develop this argument with details, examples and other possible points of view. Sum up your argument in the last paragraph. Check you have answered the question.
- Write the essay, remembering all the time the central point you are making.
- On completion, go back over what you have written to eliminate careless errors and improve expression. Read it aloud to yourself, or, if you are feeling more confident, to a relative or friend.

If you can, try to type your essay, using a word processor. This will allow you to correct and improve your writing without spoiling its appearance.

Examination essay

The essay written in an examination often carries more marks than the coursework essay even though it is written under considerable time pressure.

In the revision period build up notes on various aspects of the text you are using. Fortunately, in acquiring this set of York Notes on *Educating Rita*, you have made a prudent beginning! York Notes are set out to give you vital information and help you to construct your personal overview of the text.

Make notes with appropriate quotations about the key issues of the set text. Go into the examination knowing your text and having a clear set of opinions about it.

In most English Literature examinations you can take in copies of your set books. This is an enormous advantage although it may lull you into a false sense of security. Beware! There is simply not enough time in an examination to read the book from scratch.

In the examination

- Read the question paper carefully and remind yourself what you have to do.
- Look at the questions on your set texts to select the one that most interests you and mentally work out the points you wish to stress.
- Remind yourself of the time available and how you are going to use it.
- Briefly map out a short plan in note form that will keep your writing on track and illustrate the key argument you want to make.
- Then set about writing it.
- When you have finished, check through to eliminate errors.

To summarise, these are the keys to success:

- **Know the text**
- **Have a clear understanding of and opinions on the storyline, characters, setting, themes and writer's concerns**
- **Select the right material**
- **Plan and write a clear response, continually bearing the question in mind**

A typical essay question on *Educating Rita* is followed by a sample essay plan in note form. This does not present the only answer to the question, merely one answer. Do not be afraid to include your own ideas and leave out some of the ones in this sample! Remember that quotations are essential to prove and illustrate the points you make.

Examine Frank's growing sense of unease as Rita becomes more educated.

Part 1:
Introduction

Establish that in the early scenes, it is Frank who is in control. Look at his use of language and compare it to the way Rita speaks, showing how this partly prevents her from being fully accepted in Frank's world.

Part 2:
Rita's growing confidence

Look closely at Rita's change in character in Act II Scene 1, after attending the summer school. She tells Frank that she has already 'done' Blake. Other lecturers besides Frank have begun to have a bearing on her development. Rita also mentions Trish, who has become another influence in her life. Give examples.

Part 3:
Frank's jealousy

Look at Frank's reaction when Rita is invited to go to France with Tiger and his friends. Are the reasons he gives for her not going simply excuses? Consider the way he treats Rita when she tries to change her way of speaking (Act II Scene 2). He implores, 'Rita! Just be yourself'. Is he failing to understand that Rita does not want to be 'herself', and that she is trying to escape her situation by becoming educated?

Part 4:
Rita's 'uniqueness' disappears

Consider the way Frank becomes appalled at what he has created in Rita. Why does he liken himself to Mary Shelley who wrote the novel *Frankenstein*? He feels that she has changed, and not for the better, saying that when she writes, 'there's nothing of you in there'. When she is late for a tutorial, he asks, 'perhaps you don't want to waste your time coming here any more?' Is this a sign of Frank's own insecurity?

Part 5: Reflect on the final scene and how both characters seem
Conclusion to have come to terms with themselves and appear to be
more settled, despite the fact that neither of them is
sure what the future holds. Think about Frank's present
of the dress. Does this symbolise his acceptance that
Rita has matured into an educated woman?

FURTHER QUESTIONS

1 What does Rita gain from her 'education' and what
does she lose?

2 Compare and contrast the way Rita and Frank use
language throughout *Educating Rita*.

3 Rita describes herself as a 'half-caste' (Act I
Scene 7), neither fitting comfortably into her own
society or that of Frank. How appropriate would it
be to describe Frank in that way?

4 Look closely at Act I Scenes 6–7. Explain why
Frank invites Rita to dinner and, ultimately, why
she fails to turn up.

5 Explore Willy Russell's use of humour in the play.

6 Although *Educating Rita* is a comedy, Willy Russell
develops a number of serious issues in the play.
Select those issues which you feel are most
important and examine his treatment of them in
detail.

7 This play is about educating Rita. Frank also learns
a lot about himself, but what have you learned from
the play?

8 Is the play still as relevant today as it was when it
was first written?

9 Select the three scenes in the play which you find
most dramatic and explain why they are so
powerful.

10 As the director of the play, what ideas would you
want to put across to the audience and how would
you ensure that you were successful?

CULTURAL CONNECTIONS

BROADER PERSPECTIVES

Shirley Valentine   Compare *Educating Rita* with *Shirley Valentine*, another play written by Willy Russell. Both plays have women as their central characters and they both share a common desire to alter their mundane lives.

Cinema adaptations   Both plays have been adapted for cinema, and it is also worth comparing them on this basis. Consider the textual changes and additions which have been made by the film-makers. How is the art of the director different to that of the playwright (see Literary Terms)?

Texts within the text   The text of *Educating Rita* refers to a wide range of texts which are well worth studying in their own right. The plays of Henrik Ibsen and the novels of E.M. Forster are two such examples. Or, if you are interested in poetry, why not compare the works of William Blake with the contemporary Liverpool poet Roger McGough?

Pygmalion   Another text which has parallels with *Educating Rita* is the play by George Bernard Shaw, *Pygmalion* (also a study guide in this York Notes series). First produced in 1914 and later screened as the film *My Fair Lady*, it tells the story of a poor flower girl called Eliza Doolittle who is taken in by Professor Higgins, an expert in linguistics. He teaches her to speak 'properly' and, just like Rita, she is transformed into an entirely different character.

Frankenstein   In *Educating Rita*, Frank compares himself to Frankenstein, the man from Mary Shelley's novel of the same name, who created a monster. The novel charts the attempts of a scientist who tries to create a human being and bring it to life, but the 'monster' becomes uncontrollable. It is worth considering, therefore, how far you agree with Frank's analogy (see Literary Terms)?

analogy to suggest a likeness between two things

antithesis opposing or contrasting ideas

assonance the repitition of vowel sounds

dialect accent and vocabulary which varies due to social and regional background

irony this consists of saying one thing while you mean another, often through understatement, concealment or indirect statement

metaphor an image where something is described as being something else, not to be read literally

naturalistic in Drama, referring to the staging of a play which is essentially realistic

parody a deliberately exaggerated imitation

playwright the writer of a play

plot the storyline or main narrative thread

setting the place where the action on stage is set

stage directions advice printed in the text of a play giving instructions or information about the movements, gestures and appearance of the actors, or on the special effects required at a particular moment in the action

structure the way a work of literature has been pieced together, a framework

symbolism the practice of using symbols to represent something else

theme a repeated idea which has a prominent place in the play

tragedy a serious play which ends in misfortune

unity relating to the classical unities which governed the structure of plays, for example the unity of place which proposed that stage action should be limited to one set in order to make the play more realistic

TEST ANSWERS

TEST YOURSELF (Act I Scenes 1–4)

A 1 Roger McGough
2 Rita Mae Brown
3 E.M. Forster
4 Henrik Ibsen

TEST YOURSELF (Act I Scenes 5–8)

A 1 Denny
2 Julia
3 Macbeth
4 Rita's mother

TEST YOURSELF (Act II Scenes 1–3)

A 1 Trish
2 Tiger
3 The university authorities
4 Frank's regular students

TEST YOURSELF (Act II Scenes 4–7)

A 1 The students Rita meets at the bistro
2 Frank, talking about his own poetry
3 Trish
4 Rita

NOTES

NOTES

NOTES

NOTES

NOTES

Notes

NOTES

GCSE and equivalent levels (£3.50 each)

Maya Angelou
I Know Why the Caged Bird Sings

Jane Austen
Pride and Prejudice

Harold Brighouse
Hobson's Choice

Charlotte Brontë
Jane Eyre

Emily Brontë
Wuthering Heights

Charles Dickens
David Copperfield

Charles Dickens
Great Expectations

Charles Dickens
Hard Times

George Eliot
Silas Marner

William Golding
Lord of the Flies

Willis Hall
The Long and the Short and the Tall

Thomas Hardy
Far from the Madding Crowd

Thomas Hardy
The Mayor of Casterbridge

Thomas Hardy
Tess of the d'Urbervilles

L.P. Hartley
The Go-Between

Seamus Heaney
Selected Poems

Susan Hill
I'm the King of the Castle

Barry Hines
A Kestrel for a Knave

Louise Lawrence
Children of the Dust

Harper Lee
To Kill a Mockingbird

Laurie Lee
Cider with Rosie

Arthur Miller
A View from the Bridge

Arthur Miller
The Crucible

Robert O'Brien
Z for Zachariah

George Orwell
Animal Farm

J.B. Priestley
An Inspector Calls

Willy Russell
Educating Rita

Willy Russell
Our Day Out

J.D. Salinger
The Catcher in the Rye

William Shakespeare
Henry V

William Shakespeare
Julius Caesar

William Shakespeare
Macbeth

William Shakespeare
A Midsummer Night's Dream

William Shakespeare
The Merchant of Venice

William Shakespeare
Romeo and Juliet

William Shakespeare
The Tempest

William Shakespeare
Twelfth Night

George Bernard Shaw
Pygmalion

R.C. Sherriff
Journey's End

Rukshana Smith
Salt on the snow

John Steinbeck
Of Mice and Men

R.L. Stevenson
Dr Jekyll and Mr Hyde

Robert Swindells
Daz 4 Zoe

Mildred D. Taylor
Roll of Thunder, Hear My Cry

Mark Twain
The Adventures of Huckleberry Finn

James Watson
Talking in Whispers

A Choice of Poets

Nineteenth Century Short Stories

Poetry of the First World War

Six Women Poets

Advanced level (£3.99 each)

Margaret Atwood
The Handmaid's Tale

William Blake
Songs of Innocence and of Experience

Emily Brontë
Wuthering Heights

Geoffrey Chaucer
The Wife of Bath's Prologue and Tale

Joseph Conrad
Heart of Darkness

Charles Dickens
Great Expectations

F. Scott Fitzgerald
The Great Gatsby

Thomas Hardy
Tess of the d'Urbervilles

James Joyce
Dubliners

Arthur Miller
Death of a Salesman

William Shakespeare
Antony and Cleopatra

William Shakespeare
Hamlet

William Shakespeare
King Lear

William Shakespeare
The Merchant of Venice

William Shakespeare
Romeo and Juliet

William Shakespeare
The Tempest

Mary Shelley
Frankenstein

Alice Walker
The Color Purple

Tennessee Williams
A Streetcar Named Desire

Forthcoming Titles in the Series

Jane Austen
Emma

Jane Austen
Pride and Prejudice

Charlotte Brontë
Jane Eyre

Seamus Heaney
Selected Poems

William Shakespeare
Much Ado About Nothing

William Shakespeare
Othello

John Webster
The Duchess of Malfi

Chinua Achebe
Things Fall Apart

Edward Albee
Who's Afraid of Virginia Woolf?

Jane Austen
Mansfield Park

Jane Austen
Northanger Abbey

Jane Austen
Persuasion

Jane Austen
Sense and Sensibility

Samuel Beckett
Waiting for Godot

Alan Bennett
Talking Heads

John Betjeman
Selected Poems

Robert Bolt
A Man for All Seasons

Robert Burns
Selected Poems

Lord Byron
Selected Poems

Geoffrey Chaucer
The Franklin's Tale

Geoffrey Chaucer
The Merchant's Tale

Geoffrey Chaucer
The Miller's Tale

Geoffrey Chaucer
The Nun's Priest's Tale

Geoffrey Chaucer
Prologue to the Canterbury Tales

Samuel Taylor Coleridge
Selected Poems

Daniel Defoe
Moll Flanders

Daniel Defoe
Robinson Crusoe

Shelagh Delaney
A Taste of Honey

Charles Dickens
Bleak House

Charles Dickens
Oliver Twist

Emily Dickinson
Selected Poems

John Donne
Selected Poems

Douglas Dunn
Selected Poems

George Eliot
Middlemarch

George Eliot
The Mill on the Floss

T.S. Eliot
The Waste Land

T.S. Eliot
Selected Poems

Henry Fielding
Joseph Andrews

E.M. Forster
Howards End

E.M. Forster
A Passage to India

John Fowles
The French Lieutenant's Woman

Brian Friel
Translations

Elizabeth Gaskell
North and South

Oliver Goldsmith
She Stoops to Conquer

Graham Greene
Brighton Rock

Thomas Hardy
Jude the Obscure

Thomas Hardy
Selected Poems

Nathaniel Hawthorne
The Scarlet Letter

Ernest Hemingway
The Old Man and the Sea

Homer
The Iliad

Homer
The Odyssey

Aldous Huxley
Brave New World

Ben Jonson
The Alchemist

Ben Jonson
Volpone

James Joyce
A Portrait of the Artist as a Young Man

John Keats
Selected Poems

Philip Larkin
Selected Poems

D.H. Lawrence
The Rainbow

D.H. Lawrence
Sons and Lovers

D.H. Lawrence
Women in Love

Christopher Marlowe
Doctor Faustus

John Milton
Paradise Lost Bks I & II

John Milton
Paradise Lost IV & IX

Sean O'Casey
Juno and the Paycock

George Orwell
Nineteen Eighty-four

John Osborne
Look Back in Anger

Wilfred Owen
Selected Poems

Harold Pinter
The Caretaker

Sylvia Plath
Selected Works

Alexander Pope
Selected Poems

Jean Rhys
Wide Sargasso Sea

William Shakespeare
As You Like It

William Shakespeare
Coriolanus

William Shakespeare
Henry IV Pt 1

William Shakespeare
Henry V

William Shakespeare
Julius Caesar

William Shakespeare
Measure for Measure

William Shakespeare
Much Ado About Nothing

William Shakespeare
A Midsummer Night's Dream

William Shakespeare
Richard II

William Shakespeare
Richard III

William Shakespeare
Sonnets

William Shakespeare
The Taming of the Shrew

William Shakespeare
The Winter's Tale

George Bernard Shaw
Arms and the Man

George Bernard Shaw
Saint Joan

Richard Brinsley Sheridan
The Rivals

Muriel Spark
The Prime of Miss Jean Brodie

John Steinbeck
The Grapes of Wrath

John Steinbeck
The Pearl

Tom Stoppard
*Rosencrantz and Guildenstern
are Dead*

Jonathan Swift
Gulliver's Travels

John Millington Synge
*The Playboy of the Western
World*

W.M. Thackeray
Vanity Fair

Virgil
The Aeneid

Derek Walcott
Selected Poems

Oscar Wilde
*The Importance of Being
Earnest*

Tennessee Williams
Cat on a Hot Tin Roof

Tennessee Williams
The Glass Menagerie

Virginia Woolf
Mrs Dalloway

Virginia Woolf
To the Lighthouse

William Wordsworth
Selected Poems

W.B. Yeats
Selected Poems

York Notes – the Ultimate Literature Guides

York Notes are recognised as the best literature study guides.
If you have enjoyed using this book and have found it useful, you
can now order others directly from us – simply follow the ordering
instructions below.

HOW TO ORDER

Decide which title(s) you require and then order in one of the following
ways:

Booksellers
All titles available from good bookstores.

By post
List the title(s) you require in the space provided overleaf,
select your method of payment, complete your name and
address details and return your completed order form and
payment to:

Addison Wesley Longman Ltd
PO BOX 88
Harlow
Essex CM19 5SR

By phone
Call our Customer Information Centre on 01279 623923 to
place your order, quoting mail number: HEYN1.

By fax
Complete the order form overleaf, ensuring you fill in your
name and address details and method of payment, and fax it
to us on 01279 414130.

By e-mail
E-mail your order to us on awlhe.orders@awl.co.uk listing
title(s) and quantity required and providing full name and
address details as requested overleaf. Please quote mail
number: HEYN1. Please do not send credit card details by
e-mail.

York Notes Order Form

Titles required:

Quantity	Title/ISBN	Price

Sub total _____

Please add £2.50 postage & packing _____

(*P & P is free for orders over £50*) _____

Total _____

Mail no: HEYN1

Your Name _____

Your Address _____

_____

Postcode _____ Telephone _____

Method of payment

☐ I enclose a cheque or a P/O for £_____ made payable to Addison Wesley Longman Ltd

☐ Please charge my Visa/Access/AMEX/Diners Club card
Number _____ Expiry Date _____
Signature _____ Date _____

(please ensure that the address given above is the same as for your credit card)

Prices and other details are correct at time of going to press but may change without notice. All orders are subject to status.

☐ *Please tick this box if you would like a complete listing of Longman Study Guides (suitable for GCSE and A-level students)*

York Press

Longman

Addison
Wesley
Longman